M000287258

Mary Ann
To

Karen
From

_1 - 15 - 18_
Date

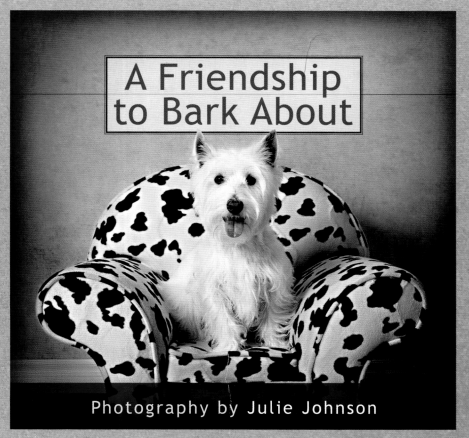

A Friendship to Bark About

Photography by Julie Johnson

HARVEST HOUSE PUBLISHERS™
EUGENE, OREGON

A Friendship to Bark About

Text copyright © 2013 by Harvest House Publishers
Photography copyright © 2013 by Julie Johnson, Vine Images

Published by Harvest House Publishers
Eugene, Oregon 97402
www.harvesthousepublishers.com

ISBN 978-0-7369-4678-0

Design and production by Garborg Design Works, Savage, Minnesota

Harvest House Publishers has made every effort to trace the ownership of all poems and quotes. In the event of a question arising from the use of a poem or quote, we regret any error made and will be pleased to make the necessary correction in future editions of this book.

All verses are taken from the Holy Bible, New Living Translation, copyright © 1996, 2004, 2007 by Tyndale House Foundation. Used by permission of Tyndale House Publishers, Inc., Carol Stream, Illinois 60188. All rights reserved.

Printed in China

13 14 15 16 17 18 19 20 21 / LP / 10 9 8 7 6 5 4 3 2 1

Pet pals and
people pals
make the world
a better place.

COMPANION

My little old dog:
A heart-beat
At my feet.
Edith Wharton

Silly

The great pleasure of a dog is that you may make a fool of yourself with him and not only will he not scold you, but he will make a fool of himself too.

Samuel Butler

My Dog! what remedy remains,
Since, teach you all I can,
I see you, after all my pains,
So much resemble man?

William Cowper

4

AMIGO

A true friend is
the gift of God,
and he only who
made hearts
can unite them.

Robert South

There is nothing on this
earth more to be prized
than true friendship.

Saint Thomas Aquinas

Whether we're on a great adventure or taking a siesta, life is a fiesta with our amigos.

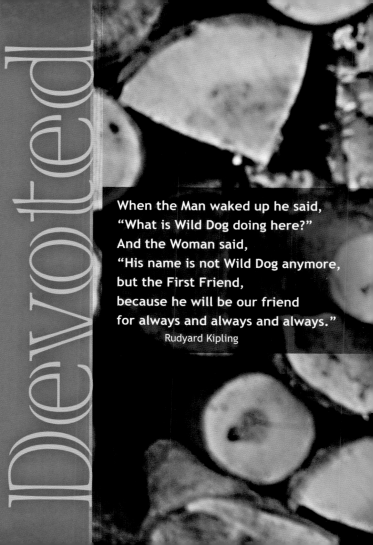

But the word "friend" does not exactly depict his affectionate worship. He loves us and reveres us as though we had drawn him out of nothing. He is, before all, our creature full of gratitude, and more devoted than the apple of our eye.

Maurice Maeterlinck,
from *Our Friend, the Dog*

Devoted

When the Man waked up he said,
"What is Wild Dog doing here?"
And the Woman said,
"His name is not Wild Dog anymore,
but the First Friend,
because he will be our friend
for always and always and always."
Rudyard Kipling

A friend is always loyal,
and a brother is born
to help in time of need.

The Book of Proverbs

When we forget what it means to be
a genuine confidante, we can look to our
four-legged friends to understand loyalty,
faithfulness, and complete discretion.

A friend is what the heart
needs all the time.

Henry Van Dyke

11

Yes, we must ever be friends;
    and of all who offer you friendship,
Let me be ever the first, the truest,
    the nearest and dearest!

Henry Wadsworth Longfellow

Best Friend

The dog has been esteemed
and loved by all the people
on earth and he has deserved
this affection, for he renders
services that have made him
man's best friend.

Alfred Barbou

A friend is one before
whom I may think aloud.

Ralph Waldo Emerson

Life education begins at birth and
continues until we've spent our lives
on those we love and on all that is dear.
Thank goodness for friends who are our
gentle, patient teachers.

Be true to your
work, your word,
and your friend.

Henry David Thoreau

Buddy

Every time I
think of you,
I give thanks
to my God.
The Book of
Philippians

I consider you
as a friend,
who will take
me just as
I am, good,
or bad, or
indifferent.
James Boswell

17

CHUM

Don't you remember when, your mother laughingly dissenting, your father said that you might have him, and with rapture in your heart and a broad smile on your face you went dancing through the town to *get* him?

There was quite a family of them—the old mother dog and her four children. Of the puppies it was hard to tell which was the best; that is, hard for the disinterested observer. As for yourself, in the very incipiency of your hesitation something about one of the doggies appealed to you. Your eyes and hand wandered to the others but invariably came back to him.

With the mother anxiously yet proudly looking on, you picked him up in your glad young arms, and he cuddled and squirmed and licked your face; and in an instant the subtle bonds of chumship were sealed forever.

Edwin L. Sabin, from *Chums*

His friends he loved.
His direst earthly foes—
Cats—I believe he did
but feign to hate.

Sir William Watson

A childhood chum helps us recall our early years with fondness and walk into our future knowing we are not alone.

Faithful

The dog is the most faithful of animals and would be much esteemed were it not so common. Our Lord God has made his greatest gift the commonest.

Martin Luther

A faithful and true friend is a living treasure.

Robert Hall

PARTNERS

A joy shared is a joy doubled.

Johann Wolfgang von Goethe

IN CRIME

Friendship improves happiness and abates misery, by the doubling of our joy and the dividing of our grief.

Cicero

Life is an enriching journey when we're making our way through the peaks and valleys with a dear friend.

UNTIL ONE HAS LOVED AN
ANIMAL, A PART OF ONE'S
SOUL REMAINS UNAWAKENED.

Anatole France

Rambunctious

The dog was
created especially
for children. He is
the god of frolic.

Henry Ward Beecher

COUNSELOR

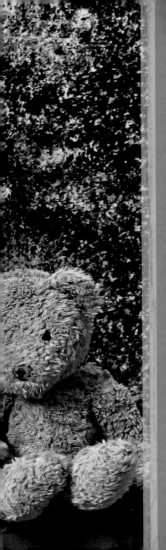

Here is no tint of mortal change; the day,—
Beneath whose light the dog and peasant-boy
Gambol, with look, and almost bark, of joy,—
Still seems, though centuries have passed, to stay.
Then gaze again, that shadowed scenes may teach
Lessons of peace and love, beyond all speech.

William Lisle Bowles, from *On a Beautiful Landscape*

A true friendship is as wise as it is tender.

Henry David Thoreau

Forever friends and dear dogs are great for a person's emotional stability. They are ever-ready counselors reminding us to be ourselves and share our hearts.

All in the town were still asleep,
When the sun came up with a shout and a leap.
In the lonely streets unseen by man,
A little dog danced. And the day began.

Rupert Brooke

There is no friend like an old friend who has shared our morning days, no greeting like his welcome, no homage like his praise.

Oliver Wendell Holmes

Playful

Those affectionate
eyes, that tail that
wags his whole body,
and the inviting
yip that says come
play, these are the
irresistible charms
of our pet dogs.

BE YOURSELF,
SIMPLE,
HONEST, AND
UNPRETENDING,
AND YOU WILL
ENJOY THROUGH
LIFE THE RESPECT
AND LOVE OF
FRIENDS.
William Sherman

A friend may well
be reckoned the
masterpiece of nature.
Ralph Waldo Emerson

CHARMING

We long for an affection
altogether ignorant of our
faults. Heaven has accorded
this to us in the uncritical
canine attachment.

George Eliot

Trusting

IF A DOG WILL NOT COME
TO YOU AFTER HAVING
LOOKED YOU IN THE FACE,
YOU SHOULD GO HOME AND
EXAMINE YOUR CONSCIENCE.

Woodrow Wilson

ATTENTIVE

I saw my little Pelléas sitting at the foot of my writing-table, his tail carefully folded under his paws; his head a little on one side, the better to question me; at once attentive and tranquil, as a saint should be in the presence of God.

Maurice Maeterlinck, from *Our Friend, the Dog*

TRUE FRIENDS VISIT US IN PROSPERITY ONLY WHEN INVITED, BUT IN ADVERSITY THEY COME WITHOUT INVITATION.

Theophrastus

The best listeners we will ever know have floppy ears, wagging tails, and wet noses.

35

It was Toto that made Dorothy laugh, and saved her from growing as gray as her other surroundings. Toto was not gray; he was a little black dog, with long, silky hair and small black eyes that twinkled merrily on either side of his funny, wee nose. Toto played all day long, and Dorothy played with him, and loved him dearly.

Frank Baum, from *The Wonderful Wizard of Oz*

Hilarious

You want a friend in this city? Get a dog.

Harry S. Truman

Life is to be fortified by many friendships. To love and to be loved is the greatest happiness of existence.

Sydney Smith

Looking into the eyes of a beloved pet, we find more than enough love and loyalty to wrap up our cares.

LOVING

Dog! When we first met on the highway of life, we came from the two poles of creation... What can be the meaning of the obscure love for me that has sprung up in your little heart?

Anatole France

39

There were ten of them—spaniels, Yorkshires, black and tans—a very regiment of tiny dogs... The combined weight of all ten of these tiny darlings, indeed, would have come well under eight pounds. But if their bodies were small, their hearts were big. They were loyal little companions, these pets of twenty years; and as I think of the many miles along life's highway that they pattered at my side, making brighter the hours by graceful prank and unfailing love, I breathe a sigh in memory of my dogs, who were my faithful little friends.

Clara Morris, from *My Dogs*

jokester

Every man should have a fair-sized cemetery in which to bury the faults of his friends.

Henry Ward Beecher

SWEET

Thus nature has no love for solitude, and always leans, as it were, on some support; and the sweetest support is found in the most intimate friendship.

Cicero

I THINK I COULD TURN AND LIVE WITH ANIMALS, THEY ARE SO PLACID AND SELF-CONTAINED.

Walt Whitman

Faithful friends are sweet blessings and joyful reminders of all that is good and right and of value in this world.

43

You are to know then, that as it is likeness that begets affection, so my favourite dog is a little one, a lean one, and none of the finest shaped... If it be the chief point of friendship to comply with a friend's motions and inclinations, he possesses this in an eminent degree: he lies down when I sit, and walks when I walk, which is more than many good friends can pretend to.

Alexander Pope

Trustworthy

You ask of my companions. Hills, sir, and the sundown, and a dog as large as myself that my father bought me. They are better than human beings, because they know but do not tell.

Emily Dickinson

COURA

The heart of animals is the foundation of their life, the sovereign of everything within them, the sun of their microcosm, that upon which all growth depends, from which all power proceeds.

William Harvey

Some friendships are made by nature, some by contract, some by interest, and some by souls.

Jeremy Taylor

When we walk together, we are stronger, more confident, and filled with courage to venture farther than we would alone.

GEOUS

Little friends
may prove
great friends.
Aesop

Dependable

MY DEAR OLD
DOG, MOST
CONSTANT OF
ALL FRIENDS.

William Croswell Doane

Soft

Why is it that the sight of a puppy always—always—brings a smile to our faces and a warm joy to our hearts?

By and by came my little puppy, and then my cup was full, my happiness was perfect. It was the dearest little waddling thing, and so smooth and soft and velvety, and had such cunning little awkward paws, and such affectionate eyes, and such a sweet and innocent face; and it made me so proud to see how the children and their mother adored it, and fondled it, and exclaimed over every little wonderful thing it did. It did seem to me that life was just too lovely...

Mark Twain, from *A Dog's Tale*

Buy a pup and your money will buy
Love unflinching that cannot lie.

Rudyard Kipling, from *The Power of the Dog*

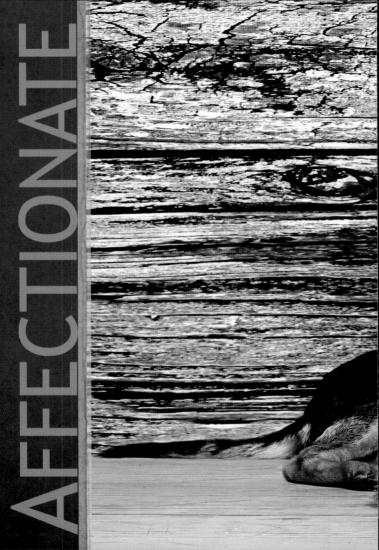

We long for an affection altogether ignorant of our faults. Heaven has accorded this to us in the uncritical canine attachment.

George Eliot

The most affectionate creature in the world is a wet dog.

Ambrose Bierce

AFFECTIONATE

Best friend, my well-spring in the wilderness!

George Eliot

Recollect that the Almighty, who gave the dog to be companion of our pleasures and our toils, hath invested him with a nature noble and incapable of deceit.

Sir Walter Scott, from *The Talisman*

SPIRITED

Watching a young pup run full-tilt along the sandy shore, one can't help but laugh out loud and call it a good day.

The more
I see of
men the
more I
like dogs.

Madame de Staël

He cannot be
a gentleman
which loveth
not a dog.

John Northbrooke

Friends are the
sunshine of life.
John Hay

No matter the day, arriving
home to a pet's enthusiastic
bark and wagging tail makes
everything oh-so-much better.

WHO FINDS A
FAITHFUL FRIEND,
FINDS A TREASURE.
Jewish Proverb

ENCOURAGER

A dog hath true love,

A dog hath right good understanding,

A wise dog knoweth all things,

A dog hath force and kindliness,

A dog hath mettle and is comely,

A dog is in all things seemly.

A knowing dog thinketh no evil,

A dog hath a memory that forgeteth not,

I say unto you again a dog forsaketh not his duty,

Hath might and cunning therewith and a great brave heart.

Gace de la Vigne

Brave

It is a friendly heart that
has plenty of friends.

William Thackeray

With unabashed devotion,
boundless energy, and a
lifetime of love, our dogs
naturally raise our spirits
and bring out the best in us.

FUN

My friend peers in on me with merry
Wise face, and though the sky stay dim,
The very light of day, the very
Sun's self comes in with him.

Algernon Charles Swinburne

A thing of beauty
is a joy forever.

John Keats

Take a walk with a dog and discover joy in the moment-by-moment experience. The new sights, sounds, and smells along the way become so much more important than the destination.

Adventure

A true friend...advises justly, assists readily, adventures boldly, takes all patiently, defends courageously, and continues a friend unchangeably.

William Penn

64